NEW BEGINNINGS

NEW BEGINNINGS

A BIPOLAR'S JOURNEY TO REGAIN HER GOD-GIVEN IDENTITY

by Faith Bonyak

Strategic Book Publishing and Rights Co.

Strategic Book Publishing and Rights Co.
12620 FM 1960, Suite A4-507
Houston, TX 77065
www.sbpra.com

ISBN: 978-1-61897-082-4

Book Design by Julius Kiskis

20 19 18 17 16 15 14 13 12   1 2 3 4 5

DEDICATION

To:

Pastor John without you I wouldn't have
found my Identity.

My circle of friends Shannon, Brandy, Sarah, Sam,
Christa, Audrey, Kellie, Christy, Merrick,
and my Renovate Family:
Having you all to lean on is like being
a super-hero nothing can hurt me.

And finally to Rev. Dr. Ed Rudiger: thank you
for "not letting go."

CONTENTS

PROLOGUE

As in every story, there are two sides to this one. I retell my stories the best I can remember them. However, given the fact that I have both bipolar disorder and borderline personality disorder, and go through many cycles, my perception of certain events may differ slightly from others who have been with me along the way. I retell these times in my life the way I remember them.

By the time this is published, many relationships that I have struggled with might be different. I don't hold anything against those who have made my life difficult to live, but it's because of their callousness and abuse that I have become the person I am today. I don't know if I exactly agree with the saying "what doesn't kill you makes you stronger," but I believe that your situation is what you make of it.

Don't read this book and feel hatred toward those who have abused me. Read this book as the journey it's meant to share. I go through and give details of the many types of identities (as I choose to call them) which I became entangled with because of circumstances life threw my way. I am still living life with these identities. I struggle, yes, for what seems like a great deal of my life, but I do have happy memories. The purpose of this book is to help

the reader understand what has come from the hardship
and the pain, and ultimately the triumph I encounter at
the end.

As an adult, I have undergone many hours of therapy and
counseling for the horrific things, I've endured. As helpful
as those sessions were, the most important reason for my
optimistic attitude, despite my issues, is my deep faith in
God. My religious beliefs have kept me going when I had
nothing else to grab and hold onto. It's because of God
that I have since found my true identity. To discover this
identity, you'll have to continue to read.

As you read about my journey, be assured that everything
works out. For me it's not how the journey ends that is
miraculous, but how all the stories in between have made
the journey so worthwhile. My hope for this book is that
it will spark a want for a new beginning in those that read
it, knowing that if I could make it through my trials, there
is hope for you.

PART 1

Identities

Chapter 1
THE SICK ARMY BRAT

Throughout our lives, we take on a variety of identities. As people, we change, and as we do, we adopt a new identity. Seldom do we carry the same one throughout our lives.

Of course, our identities at the beginning of life are pretty much the same infant, toddler, and so forth. Even at these early stages of development, we all display various characteristics that make us unique.

For as long as I can remember, I was identified as "the sick one." My chronic ear problems really made me stand out among my peers. There were times when I would miss school for weeks because of surgeries and various other hospitalizations. On top of missing school for being sick, I missed solidifying my relationships because my family moved quite a bit, due to my dad's affiliation with the military. In my absence, other children made friends. Each time I returned, I became the outsider looking in. I was never given a good chance to learn how to interact with other kids. The attention I received after coming home from across the world was short lived and made me feel segregated from everyone else. Soon I was alone, and most of the time, I was sick.

In a desperate attempt to try and shield me from contracting any other illnesses, my parents overprotected me. In the winter, I was seldom permitted to play in the snow. When I was given the opportunity, it was only for short periods of time. Although I know my parents were looking out for my best interest, it came with a pretty hefty price tag.

I lost any real ability to interact socially with my peers. As a result, I was often clingy, and as the metaphor goes, "I followed people around like a lost puppy." I was so desperate to have friends to call my own, I would resort to many different tactics. I would do whatever other kids asked. I remember sitting on a picnic table outside on the playground when one of the girls I was attempting to make friends asked me to say all the swear words I could think of to show that I wasn't a "tattle tale." I did just that. I didn't even know how many of them were real swear words, but I was willing to do anything.

If I learned of someone's birthday, I knew I had to do something special for that person. I knew there was no way my family could afford for me to buy a present for all these folks. A birthday for someone I really wanted to impress was reason to scour my room and the house for anything of interest to take to school and give away. It had to be small enough to fit into my backpack to avoid suspicion, so my mom wouldn't know what I was doing.

The worst part was that I allowed myself to be treated badly, just so I didn't have to be alone. The memory that haunts me the most is the one about two girls, whom I admired, that decided they needed a pet. I became their dog. My hair was down to my waist at the time, and I wore it in a ponytail. They grabbed me by the ponytail and dragged me across the playground. It hurt so much. When we passed the teacher on recess duty, the girls just said, "She's okay, she's our puppy," and that was the end of it. I had to decide to either tell them I wouldn't be their puppy anymore and be by myself or endure it. I decided that at least they were playing with me, so when they wanted me I endured the pain.

To make matters worse, I was straddled with a second identity: "the army brat."

This added identity brought change. I could start over with fresh new faces and really do things right. However, things did not quite work out as I had planned.

When my family moved to Germany for the last time, it was the summer before I would start third grade. I was anxious to make as many friends as possible. School started, and I was ready to go!

At the start of any school year, my mom provided my teachers an accurate history of my condition. To accommodate my hearing problems, she asked that I be seated at the front of the classroom. During the first few weeks of school, this small accommodation was adequately followed. Soon, my math grades began to slip, and I was constantly being reprimanded for talking. In truth, I couldn't hear what she was saying, so I was getting the information from my neighbor, although the more I got in trouble, the less he wanted to help. In an effort to teach me a lesson, the teacher moved me to the back table where I sat by myself.

Being moved away from my peers added to my dilemma and just compounded my need for acceptance and friendship. Not one of these kids wanted to be associated with the girl who had to sit by herself.

Now that my identities had crossed paths, my life was becoming increasingly more difficult to manage. It is very trying to break free from the molds my identities held me to. I struggled so often, with those things that identified me but were no longer an accurate description of who I truly am. Who I say I am, is never who I want to be.

In trying to discover who we want to be, we go on journeys. We go searching for an appropriate identity. We try on many different identities to see what fits with whom we are interacting with at that time in our lives. We slowly develop relationships based on how well they've developed in our childhood. As adults, we tend to model our relationships based on what we saw and lived as children.

An adult who truly believed I was no one cut my journey short. I was told I was "no one" for a long time. It was not long after hearing those words that I started to acknowledge that person's theories of me as truth. From then on, those first two identities no longer suited me. A family member who was about to re-enter my life had something different in mind.

Chapter 2

THE WORTHLESS VICTIM

My family's journey to Germany was cut short. My grandmother's third husband was ill and not expected to live much longer. The army granted my family an emergency leave to return home to West Virginia. During our deployment to Germany, we had rented out our house in West Virginia to friends from our church, so my family was staying at my grandmother's house.

This increase in family time was something new to me. My mom's siblings had come for the funeral, but I did not go. I barely knew the man, and I wasn't old enough to really understand what was happening. I was happy to spend time with cousins I never got to see. My aunts and uncles were doting over my brothers, sister, and me. To me, no one really acted as if they were grieving, but I was having fun. I didn't want to leave, because I knew that once my time there ended, we would be going back to Germany, and I would have to face that classroom. I was hoping this fun time would somehow last as long as possible.

Eventually the services were over, and the house became quiet. I was getting myself geared up for the long trip home, by airplane, train, and car, back to our apartment in Germany, when I realized that my parents were not in a hurry to get back to Berlin.

My mom, knowing her mother did not have other children living close, decided that my grandmother still needed her. However, my dad could not care for the four children himself. Together, they reached the agreement that my sister and I would remain stateside with my mom and grandmother, while my two brothers traveled back across the ocean to Germany. This one decision changed the whole course of my life. Living with my grandmother was going to be a huge change for all of us.

When I was first informed of the change in plans, I was disappointed. I would not be given the opportunity to say good-bye to the friends I had made, but the more I thought about it, the better it sounded. I had high hopes for this sudden variation. However, it didn't take long before those hopes were quickly dashed.

My grandmother was the only grandparent I had ever known. My dad's parents had died long before he ever met my mom. I guess my love and devotion to her was so extreme because she was the only grandparent I had. My grandmother knew I had no other grandparents. I guess to her it was my tough luck, because living with her turned out to be the most horrifying, eye-opening experience of my life.

As the rest of the family went on with the rest of their lives, I was beginning to enter the world of my newest identity: "the worthless victim." Up to that point, I had no real concrete memories of my grandmother and me together, but the next eighteen months would be ones I would never forget.

Immediately I began seeing that I was being treated differently in comparison to my baby sister, who was five at the time. When we were given our bedroom assignments, I was terribly shocked that my sister was given the twin-sized bed in my grandmother's room that had been vacated after our grandfather's death. My grandmother's room was pretty much set up in the theme of the Flintstone's. Of course, my grandmother would keep her own bed; she and my sister would now be roommates. That left the two attic rooms for my mother and me. Seeing how I was the youngest, I got the smaller of the two rooms that came complete with a twin bed and one sheet. My mom took the larger room with the queen-sized bed just across the way. I felt safer knowing my mom was in the room right next to me, and I decided the arrangement wouldn't be so bad after all.

I didn't mind sleeping in the attic. I had suspected I would sleep there from the get go, but there was something wrong with my mom sleeping up there instead of my sister. I discovered later that my mom would go down and sleep on the couch where it was warmer; meanwhile I got only a cover sheet and a pillow.

Besides the sleeping arrangements, the chores were also one-sided. I had to make all the beds, bring up the laundry from the basement, and help my grandmother scrub the kitchen floors. My sister, while all of this was going on, would be snuggled up on the couch in the living room watching TV.

At the tender age of eight, I made the mistake of asking my grandmother why my sister was never made to do any chores. This inquiry triggered a beating. She grabbed the wooden rolling pin and began to hit me on the back, the legs, and butt. During this lashing, she hit me so hard that she dropped the rolling pin. Having no weapon, she began to kick my body across the floor.

After it was over, and I stopped crying, she informed me that she didn't owe an eight year old an explanation about how she ran her house. She went on to say that she could tell I wasn't going to amount to anything of great importance.

"You're worthless. God could never love someone like you. You're nothing special."

I never again questioned her sense of fairness.

Life in that house pretty much stayed the same. If my mom was home with us, things remained relatively calm. Once my mom left the house for errands, or appointments, my hell would begin again.

The summer after we began living there, my mom became a camp counselor, and she and my sister were gone for a whole week. Even though my sister was gone, I was not permitted to sleep downstairs, in her bed.

During that week, I was starved, not permitted to go out to play, and beaten for any small infraction. On really bad days, she locked me in a small attic cubby space that could not be opened from the inside. It was dark and very lonely. When my mom and sister returned it was hard to contain my relief, but I had now become wary of everyone.

I already had a false sense of what a healthy relationship consisted of as demonstrated by my relationships with the kids at school. My reactions to things became extreme, and when my mom returned home, I acted as though I hadn't seen her in months as opposed to just seven days. I really felt as if her presence would save me from my grandmother until I realized that my mom and her mother didn't have a healthy relationship either. My mom would witness some degree of the abuse I endured as a child, and from my point of view, did nothing to stop it.

A shadow of resentment began to grow inside of me. I often thought to myself, my mom knows what is happening to me, yet she says nothing to stop the pain that grandma has been causing me. I must be doing something wrong or else my mom would be defending me.

I became withdrawn. My resentment toward my mom and baby sister was growing. I had been brooding for a long time about how all of this had come about. As this resentment festered, it grew into a silent rage that boiled inside of me like a pressure cooker. Once I reached my boiling point, there was no telling what was going to happen next. All of these feelings were new to me, and I didn't know what was happening. My life was changing quickly, and these hateful, self-destructive emotions took hold of my mind and thoughts on a regular basis. They finally surfaced in a tangible form.

One night I woke up from what I think was a fugue state. I was in my grandmother's room, standing beside her bed with a knife held in the air above her body. Thoughts began to race through my head faster than I could process them. Was I watching a TV show? This couldn't be me? What was I really intending to do with this knife? Would someone stop me? Even when I realized what I was doing, I did not immediately withdraw the knife. At eight years old, I was seriously weighing the pros and cons of stabbing my own grandmother. I vividly remember thinking about how long I would have to go to jail. If I told the authorities what she was doing to me, maybe they would be grateful the world was rid of her and just send me to a place where I could get help. Then the angel on my shoulder started to speak to me

"The Holy Bible says that murder is wrong, even if

the person did something wrong. She may be wrong for abusing you, but two wrongs don't make a right. You should pray for her and ask God what to do. Do you really think God will allow you into heaven knowing you stabbed your grandmother?"

Even if I thought I wouldn't go to heaven, I was really asking myself whether I could continue to live with her way of life. I decided that murder wasn't the answer. As I withdrew from her room and put the knife back precisely where I found it, I still felt that if I didn't do something, I was going to explode. That is the moment I decided to start mutilating myself.

Chapter 3
THE CUTTER

Today, cutting is something many people know about, but very few really seem to understand. For those that don't understand, let me give you a little background. Cutting is not done to get attention. It is an escape from a painful trauma or ongoing abuse. Especially for children in early adolescence, handling such abuse becomes too emotional to handle on the inside. As a way of allowing the pain and shame of the trauma to escape, people cut themselves or use any number of forms of self-mutilation. Cutting, despite popular opinion, is not an attempt at suicide. There have been times when cutters have been too enthusiastic and injured themselves much more dramatically than they had initially anticipated. A cutter really needs to speak to a professional. More times than not, someone who is cutting feels like no one will understand, and they are alone in their plight.

When I started cutting, I didn't have the frame of mind to use sharp implements such as knives, razor blades, or cutting tools. When I began to mutilate myself, I used erasers. I would take an eraser and rub my skin until it became raw and bloody. There was even times that I thought I could tattoo myself. I would erase my skin and pick at it in the hopes that it would turn into a permanent scar. Many of my scars have faded over time, but cutting is still a behavior that I deal with, even in my adulthood.

There are several times when I remember actually hurting myself. One that sticks out the most was one night when I was at church for our weekly youth service. We were in the worship part of the service, and I just began to scratch and scratch the back of my hand, which began to sting. The more it stung, the harder I would scratch. I always wore long-sleeve shirts that were too big for me, so hiding it was simple. Part of the thrill of cutting was the knowledge that I could hide it from my parents and those around me. No one would understand the impulse I had to harm myself. When I wasn't home alone, I would take any opportunity I had. I even pulled out my hair and hit myself in the head. Some days I was just so overwhelmed, I couldn't do anything but scratch at myself and claw at my skin. It was like something inside of me was trying to get out.

The newness of that thrill was short-lived, and I graduated from erasers to safety pins and superglue. I would puncture my flesh just barely under the skin and rip the safety pin out. Once the pin was out, I would pick off the excess skin, and for a while, this worked wonders. There were a couple of days at school that I had to have my hands wrapped because the wounds would start to bleed. To add to this thrill, I started to superglue my fingers together and rip them apart. These self-destructive actions seemed to keep my murderous thoughts under wraps.

Living with my grandmother everyday was really difficult. Each time I saw I her, I wanted to run to her and tell her how much I loved her and that I didn't understand why all of this was happening to me. I wanted to hit her and slap her and kick her and do all of the things she was doing to me, but I didn't. I suffered in silence. I cried myself to sleep so many times just wanting to be loved.

I knew, though, that I would not be able to keep this dark secret to myself much longer. The more I mutilated myself, the harder it was to hide. On some level, I really believed that the longer I hid my actions, the more I was lying to my mom and those I trusted. I just knew that there was no one who would understand why I did this. At my age, I really believed I was the only person who wanted to feel pain. What I was doing was not a normal reaction to things, and I had decided that it was best that I just keep it to myself. At least I wasn't thinking about killing anyone else. The mutilating was doing what I needed it to do.

My identities were all starting to come together and work against me. I was still having difficulties with my ears, and my dad was still in the military. I didn't know when he would be home, and my grandmother's actions were causing me to hurt myself on a fairly regular basis. The stress of dealing with three identities at once was becoming more than I could handle. They all seemed to be feeding off one another. The stress ran through me, causing havoc with my body's decreased ability to ward off illness, and soon I was back in the hospital.

Since being there put me out of commission and kept me from venting, I simply returned to the frame of mind that I was a worthless piece of skin. Keeping this thought in my head has been the driving force behind my injurious tendencies. The only interesting part about the whole scene was how I was able to keep it to myself. This was the one part of me that no one could take away; it all works on the assumption that it stays a secret.

The nursing staff at the hospital ruined that assumption for me. At my young age, I underestimated the knowledge that the medical personnel had about these violent acts. I really believed that I was the only one in the world hurting myself intentionally. I believed I was so worthless that I had to injure myself! Surely no one else does this, I often thought.

While another nurse started my IVs, the main nurse took my mom aside and had a conference with her out of earshot. The nurse told my mom that she had noticed the scars on my hands and forearms and asked her if she knew how those wounds came to be. My mom told her that she knew about the injuries, and it was just a phase I was going through. The nurse gently told my mom it was not a phase that I was just going to snap out of. She advised my mom to have me see a therapist, because what I was doing was a sign of emotional and physical abuse.

My mom acknowledged the concern and assured the nurse that once I was discharged, she would definitely look into getting me some therapy.

I did begin therapy, though not as soon as I was discharged; it seemed to take several months before I saw anyone. My mom took me to several therapists but kept it a secret, because my grandmother would have found it odd that I was attending therapy for abuse that she didn't believe she was committing. I also believe that my mom could not find it in herself to be truthful with her mother. I began to see that my mom had her own issues with her mother. Although the therapists explained to my mom just how grave my situation was, as soon as one of them advised my mother to remove me from my grandmother's house, so I could begin the healing process, my mom would abruptly cease treatment. Each time we left a therapist's office, my mom was warned that if I weren't removed from my present situation, my self-mutilating behaviors would not stop and would continue to escalate. Many times on the way home from therapy, my mother would barrage me with questions about what I discussed with the therapist. I told her that what I discussed was private, and I was told that I didn't have to tell anyone anything, not even my mom.

My mom didn't like hearing that. I gathered she was more afraid of what I said about her than anything else. She felt powerless and probably a bit guilty, and she wanted to know just how much guilt I was placing on her for the whole situation. To be truthful, I was more concerned about why this was happening and why I wasn't being taken out of such a hurtful place.

Instead of heeding the advice of those therapists, my mom chose to take me to spiritual counseling with the pastors of my church. I am not altogether sure why, but we stopped going there as well.

It didn't matter that I stopped going, because now my secret was out. Many people now knew that I was unstable. What little friends I had were now beginning to desert me, just like everyone else. I would almost always end up sitting by myself at my youth's church service.

My mom liked to get to our Sunday evening services a bit early to do some meditative prayer. This gave me ample time to decide where I wanted to sit. The youth of the church had a section they all sat in. I would place my things in the pew and then watch as other church members came in and chose their seats. Inevitably, before the service started, I would need to use the restroom. I would leave my belongings on the seat, but when I returned, I would find my things moved several pews away, and the rest of the youth members packed into the pew where I had chosen to sit. This did not just happen once or twice; it was like a demented dance I would do with the other youth members. Eventually, I just got tired of this treatment.

I made a decision: they would no longer move my things. To change that behavior, I started using the restroom as soon as I got there and then found my seat. I remained firmly planted in that seat. This did not deter them. They would do one of two things: pack the pew so full of kids that I was being squashed to a point where I had no choice but to move or ignore my presence by sitting several pews away from me; either way I was alone.

Back during this time, bullying was never dealt with. It was something you had to just endure. Many times my parents would say, "What doesn't kill ya makes ya stronger!" That didn't make me feel better. My life was crumbling. Home wasn't safe; church wasn't safe. The only safe harbor was school, and even that turned into another one of my personal circles of hell.

Chapter 4
THE SUICIDAL INTROVERT

After all, I had been through, I still demonstrated a pretty positive attitude, but it was just a façade. I only appeared to be happy. I kept my depression under wraps. Cutting was now a daily thing. My mom was checking my arms, so I had to change where I took out my frustration, anger, and sadness. While at school, I would punch bathroom walls until my knuckles were black and blue. That was an injury that I could easily explain away.

Like wild animals, human predators can smell blood, sweat, and fear. I guess I was oozing a vulnerability that male predators around me were waiting to feed on. Whoever said middle school years are the worst in a child's life was telling the honest to God's truth.

For the first time, the school bus was the perfect place for these predators to pounce. There was no exit. Even if I escaped to another seat, the boys would know exactly where I was and then move in for the kill. As I sat, huddled in my bus seat, I kept my eyes gazing forward and always looked out the window. I wished I could make myself invisible, but I never did achieve that power.

One by one, four older boys would surround my seat. One would sit with me while the others sat in close proximity either in the seat behind or the seat in front. This made their communication much easier. Trying to break the ice, they would engage me in frivolous conversation. All too soon, the chatter became vulgar and sexually explicit. I understood some things they said, but at other times, I was baffled. One boy would put his hand down my shirt, while another would have his hand between my legs. Once they were finished, the others, who had been waiting and watching took the opportunity to abuse me as well.

The abuse on the bus wasn't enough, and it began to happen during school time. One or two of the boys would come to my class and say that I was needed in the main office to speak with the principal. I dreaded hearing the door to the classroom open. Those voices were as hard to hear, as swallowing shards of glass would be going down my throat.

Reluctantly, I would leave my seat and walk into the hallway. The boys guided me to the boys' restroom and once inside pinned me against the wall. They forced me to touch them and eventually perform oral sex. This only happened three to four times, but the abuse on the bus continued regularly.

By now, these predators were so comfortable with the fact that their secret was safe that they started to place demands on me. I was told when I was to wear skirts; this would provide them easy access to what they wanted.

True to form, the longer the abuse went on, the less socially acceptable I became. Many of the boys responsible even bragged at how "easy" I was. Some boys went on to date my classmates and boasted to the girls about what I let them do to me.

In the eighth grade, I sat beside a boy who had abused

me before. Our teacher had the desks arranged in a position where we were in clumps with our desks facing each other. This boy sat directly to my right and spent most of the day feeling in between my legs. He too demanded I wear skirts to provide less complicated access to my body.

As a way to make my private humiliation more public, a girl who was dating the boy abusing me started a rumor that I was a lesbian. This was a truly devastating blow. Not only was I forced to deal with ongoing humiliation, but, also, a girl, who had been in my class and up until the previous year my best friend, was spreading gossip and lies about me. The rumor spread like wildfire. Everyday, I would just look at the ground and never make eye contact with anyone. I didn't feel safe anywhere.

On top of it all, the girls spreading the rumor about my sexual orientation decided they would make life a bit more interesting for me. To them, I should not have existed, but I did. To help me understand I was not wanted, they made up a catch phrase to push me away from their area. Like the rumor, this catch phrase caught on just as fast. If anyone wanted to keep me at arm's length, all they had say was "dildo," and I would no longer be any danger to them. I could barely walk down the hallway without hearing that ugly word. I was becoming even more isolated. The teachers were even listening to the rumors and started seating me in the back, so I couldn't be a danger to anyone during class time.

This new seating arrangement started to take its toll. My grades were slipping, because I couldn't hear from where I was seated. At night, what filled my mind was the image of those taunting me, and that ugly word, which echoed in my dreams all night.

At this stage of my life, other than the abuse, I knew nothing of sex or erotic terms. "Dildo" kept replaying in my mind. I didn't know what it meant, so after months of torture, I decided to casually broach the subject with my mom. Hindsight is 20/20, and boy, I can now see what a terribly bad idea that was.

One afternoon when I got home from school, I got the gumption to ask my mom about that word. I tried to soften her up with a little idle chitchat about my day at school. I decided that there was no easy way to go about this. I went in for the direct approach, hoping that it would come off as normal curiosity.

"Mom, I wanted to know if you know what a dildo is."

Never answering my question, my mom began to drill me about how I had heard that word. Crying and afraid, I told her the whole story of being called a lesbian and how that awful word was used to keep me from endangering anyone. Leaving me alone, my mom immediately called up that girl's mom. While on the phone, my classmate's mom said that it was the other way around. My mom had now had enough. She called the school and discussed what needed to be done. Of course now, I can't tell her about the boys. On top of everything else, I was in for some deep ramifications as a result of my mom's attempt at fixing the situation.

School the next day was really harsh. My classmate had passed the word around about my mom's rampage and her attempt to make sure my harassment stopped. No one talked to me. Now I was getting shoved into lockers, and my hair was being pulled from behind. At lunch, there was nowhere for me to sit. I dumped my lunch into the garbage and spent the lunch period in a lonely bathroom stall.

Considering all I had endured, i was done! I was done with pain and guilt and really done with life. I went into the kitchen, got one of my mom's cooking knives, and hid it outside behind my favorite tree. I was going to slit my wrists, and my pain would finally end. My plan never took place, but I was on the brink of exploding if I didn't catch a break.

"The suicidal introvert" was the longest identity I dealt with. It is really hard to pull yourself out of that dark place. My cutting got really bad. I began to wear black clothes, even in the summer. I would wear sweatpants and sweatshirts. I didn't have much energy for anything.

The start of my senior year was supposed to be a turning point, but it almost became the point of no return. I vowed to myself that I was not about to let anyone ruin my last year. With this vow came a whole new attitude. I know now in looking back that I had gone through a manic stage. Nothing at all could hurt me. For the first time in my life, all my previous identities came back, and they were working as a team.

Senior year was definitely a year for me to remember. Show Choir was my obsession. I had been in this class the two previous years, but this year I was determined to be Show Choir president. I had many friends in choir, and I knew this was my year. Well, it turned out fate had other plans. My coveted spot as president was given to a classmate known for finding ways to get what she wanted. However, even despite this setback, I was determined to remain optimistic.

Along with Show Choir, I was heavily involved in my drama class, and I even had my first serious relationship. For the purpose of this book, we'll call him Steve.

Steve was like no one I had ever met. He was handsome and a genius. In our final year, we spent a lot of time on the phone getting to know each other. We had so much in common, and I finally felt that I was in the right place at the right time.

My mom was getting increasingly less tolerant of the time I spent on the phone, especially with someone whom I see each day in school. Steve was my escape from reality. Soon he became my world. Seeing as though I had very little experience with love relationships, Steve ultimately became my obsession. I was willing to die if that is what it took to gain his love.

Life at home was becoming more and more intolerable. I started to find my diary in a different place than where I usually put it. I had a sneaking suspicion that my mom was reading my private thoughts, which could be very dangerous. I started carrying it with me to school until the threat of her reading it was over.

At night, when I was supposed to be asleep, I was actually suffering in silence from terrible insomnia. Through the walls, I even heard my mom comment that I had been a mistake. I rushed to call Steve. Just like all the other times, the more we talked the better I began to feel. Without any warning, my mom burst in, yelling at me to get off the phone. Almost at the same time I was hanging up the phone, my mom grabbed it from my hands. I turned away from her and the next thing I knew, I felt excruciating pain in my back; my mom had used my phone as a weapon.

The next day at school, Steve, who was very worried, came and embraced me. As I pulled away wincing, he knew I was injured. A friend of mine took me to the bathroom, and there we found a rather large bruise where my mom had used my phone against me. I knew I needed to get away for good. This time I would succeed. I was devising my escape plan.

If you add up all my risk factors for potentially committing suicide, I really should have found a way to off myself by now. When I said all my past identities were all working as a team, it is true. The previous story of my mom's fury was near my time for graduation. Two days prior, she was out of town for a women's spiritual conference. I knew this would be my only chance, but I still had one more chance to save myself: Senior Awards Night.

If I could come away with something, no matter how small, then maybe that would be enough for me to see I had become something, that I could become something to someone. This was a do or die night literally.

My dad accompanied me to the awards night. By the end of the night, I had nothing more to show for my work than what I had come in with. That was the deciding moment. I wouldn't live to see graduation.

The sound of silence all but engulfed the car ride home. In my head, I so wanted to make my last few hours with him as memorable as I could. The more I thought about it, the less I wanted to say for fear he could read my thoughts. I wasn't going to change my mind. My death was an inevitable situation. I pitied my dad. I knew my absence would hurt him deeply. Even so, it must happen as planned.

By the time we arrived home, I knew what I was going to do. After my father and my sister had gone to bed, I would get a knife from the kitchen, say one last prayer to God, and then slit my wrists. I would lie on the floor and let all my pain and guilt drain from my body.

I did exactly as I had planned. I started by saying good

night to my dad and my sister. Then, like a ton of bricks, it hit me. I couldn't leave without saying good-bye to Steve. I could come back to the knife after I was done talking.

Standing in a room, covered by a blanket of blackness, I dialed Steve's phone number one last time. Steve's dad answered. I promised him that this wouldn't take long; it wouldn't be like so many of our previous talks. Steve's dad yelled to him to pick up the extension. Once I heard the click that signified his dad had hung up, I began a final good-bye to my love.

"Good-bye my love." Those three words somehow signaled to him that this was something he hadn't anticipated.

My relationship with Steve was terribly emotional. To impress him, I began starving myself. I wanted to be perfect for him so he would never leave me.

For the past several months, he watched my weight drop quickly, and now he knew what I planned to do. "What would you do to save me if you were the only one who could?" I asked. If Steve had any questions about where this conversation was leading, it was now made crystal clear. He did, everything he could to save me. I didn't know he had his own plan.

Our talk was becoming more and more drawn out, much more so than I had originally planned. If I was going to kill myself, it had to be now. Since I was on the phone with Steve and he was not going to let me put down the phone, I had to improvise.

I grabbed a pair of scissors that I had been using for my senior English project, and I thrust them into my abdomen. This wasn't working, so I tried to slit my wrists with the inside blade. My wrists began to bleed, but not in the way

I was intending. In a fit of rage and desperation, I shoved them down my throat. Once they were lodged there, I tried opening and closing them. I was hoping beyond hope that they would cut something, ending my pain forever.

During all this, Steve was still hanging on the line. He talked to me, unaware that I was no longer listening. He knew I was doing something, and he didn't like that. Everything he said was a question that needed to be answered. He patiently waited for my responses and when he didn't get any, he began to reminisce about our relationship. Through his talking, I never got the feeling he was splitting his focus.

In the midst of my not answering him, he had been having a written conversation with his dad. He notified his dad that I was trying to kill myself, and he wasn't sure what I was doing to make that happen, but that I needed help right away. I'm sure, in a flurry of adrenaline, his dad made his way to the neighbor's house and dialed 911. Steve had given his dad explicit directions to my house and told him to ask the police not to use lights or sirens. He believed this would further drive my attempt.

I was completely caught off guard when I saw four state-police cars drive up to my house and park. I felt fear in the pit of my stomach. Things had gotten way out of hand. My problems turned from how I was going to die without waking my family to how I was going to get police officers off my lawn without anyone else finding out. If my dad or sister woke up, how could I explain the presence of eight troopers on my lawn at 2:00 a.m.? I hung up the phone without saying anything else to Steve.

I dressed in layers, long sleeves, and a coat, to cover the obvious cuts on my wrists, and to hide the blood dripping from my abdomen. I calmly explained that there must have been a misunderstanding. As they came closer and closer, I would step back so they couldn't see the blood in my mouth. They talked to me for a while and at the end gave me the card for the suicide hotline. As they left, I felt relief that I handled this without incident. Killing myself would just have to wait.

I would go to graduation rehearsal tomorrow and think of something else. I went to bed thankful that I didn't have to explain any of this to my dad or sister.

Chapter 5
THE BLACK SHEEP LIAR

That night was one of the longest of my life. Once I got back inside, I threw away the bloody clothes I was wearing and put that trash bag in the can in our basement. I cleaned up any evidence of my suicide attempt and got ready for bed. By this time, it was already 4:30 a.m. I got into bed and fell asleep; thankfully, I had gotten away with it.

My sister rudely disturbed my peaceful sleep. She barged into my room screaming and yelling. Once I finally awoke, I began to understand her tirade.

"The cops!! What were the cops doing here?"

After hearing all the yelling, my dad walked in to find out what the commotion was about. My worst fear was playing out right before my eyes. As my dad entered my room, my sister proceeded to tell him how everyone in our neighborhood knew that there were cops on our lawn last night. Several of our neighbor's homes were equipped with police scanners, and they got the call when the police were dispatched to our residence.

I had to think of something quick. I improvised a story that one of Steve's neighbors had called, thinking there was a domestic violence issue. I informed him that when they showed up, I went out and talked with them to correct the apparent misunderstanding.

My little allegory, though false, seemed to suffice. I knew in my heart this story would not stand the test of time. I had to get out. My mom would be home that evening, and I could not run the risk of having to explain this all again to her. I called Steve and asked if I could stay with his family. His dad agreed. I packed a bag and told my dad I didn't know when I'd be back.

Since I was not at home when my mom returned that Friday evening, I have no idea what chaos ensued once she learned I was gone.

I had absolutely no intention of going back. I liked Steve's family. They really showed me an outpouring of love and support that I've never known. It was fun to be getting ready for graduation with his family. I felt at peace.

Saturday morning, in the midst of all the excitement for the day, I received a phone call. This was the phone call I had been dreading. It was my mom. My mom knew nothing of the last couple day's events. I am sure that after receiving the sketchy update of my run-in with the state troopers, she must have been scared. I took a deep breath, and answered this phone call.

"Faith? What's going on?"

I just told her that I had to leave and that she and my dad would not understand what I was going through. We went back and forth for a little while, but didn't get anywhere. Finally, she gave the ultimatum I wasn't expecting.

"Faith, either you come home and get ready for graduation here at home, or none of your family will be attending the ceremony."

I went blank. I did not anticipate this turn of events. I had a very scary decision to make, one that did not come easy.

"I'm staying here," I said, and then hung up the phone.

Steve's dad had been standing next to me throughout the whole exchange. When I hung up, I collapsed into his arms and bawled for what seemed like hours. I gathered myself and relayed the conversation to Steve and his dad. Was she really serious? Would my family really miss seeing me graduate?

My parents did not attend my commencement, and neither did my sister. However, as I walked across the platform to receive my diploma, I heard cheering from the audience and realized that my brother had driven seven hours to watch me graduate.

After the ceremony, I met up with my brother who was with my cousin, her mom, and my adoptive grandmother. None of them looked particularly thrilled. To make matters worse, they informed me that my dad was not doing well emotionally, and they might end up having to take him to the hospital if he couldn't settle down. I felt horrible about the state I had left my dad in, but staying would have been worse for me.

Steve, my brother, and I went to a local restaurant to talk about how to get me to return home. My brother tried every bribe in the book, but I stayed firm in my position. If I wasn't the black sheep before, I sure was now.

I remained at Steve's for the duration of the summer. At one time, my mom came over and tried to work out an arrangement for my return. I felt as though she was treating me like a hostage and not someone who was capable of making informed decisions. In her mind, Steve's parents were holding me hostage. I am still unsure if my suicide attempt was ever brought up, but my mom left without me and without any inkling of when I'd return.

As August rolled around, Steve was preparing to head off to college. My life was still up in the air. The time had come for me to do what I'd been dreading: return to my home and face the music.

My return was not met with cheers or applause. On the contrary, I faced a silence that I've never experienced before. My sister ignored me, my mom talked to me only when she had to, and my dad had already left for his next job. I felt relieved that he wasn't there when I got home. Seeing the pain in his eyes would have been too much for me to bear.

When I returned home, my weight loss had become obvious to my mom. She was now positive that I was starving myself. My weight prior to leaving was about 180 pounds. When I left Steve's house, I was 123 pounds. I went from a size 12 to a size 6.

Mealtime was such a hassle. My mom made me sit at the table until my plate was empty. For a while, I was able to wait it out, but before long, I began to throw up my meals. My mom was over her head dealing with a daughter who had an eating disorder. My mom took me to the ER. She explained she wanted me institutionalized to help me with my disorder, and I was committed to the psychiatric ward at Chestnut Ridge.

In the fourteen days I spent there, I was diagnosed with manic depression and placed on Prozac. I also discovered I had gallstones and my gallbladder needed to be removed.

After I was discharged, we started the ball rolling on my surgery. Steve joined my mom and I the day of the surgery and stayed with me. After my surgery, Steve and I had one more day to spend together before he left for college. We broke up before he left.

Due to both of my hospitalizations, I missed the cut off for fall registration and would not begin my college life until the next spring. I was overdue for a change of scenery and was just itching to start a new life.

Chapter 6
THE COLLEGE DRUGGIE

In the early stages of college life, my parents took turns transporting me to college and picking me up, because I still did not have a driver's license. Thanks to the diagnosis of manic depression, the state of West Virginia paid for my education.

Not long after I started school, I was introduced to a girl that I began to carpool with. It was nice to not have my parents always watching me. I would soon turn nineteen and desperately wanted independence.

At the end of the semester, I was finally able to get my driver's license. Now I could take the car that was bought for me and move out. At first, I just took some clothes and planned to come back for the rest of my belongings, after I found a place to rent. When I left home, my family did not know I didn't have a place to live.

The car I had been driving broke down because of a hole in the oil pan. It was unusable. Now I'd have to walk everywhere. I just parked the car on the street. Since the weather was still warm, I didn't figure homelessness to be too terrible. I spent many nights sleeping underneath a friend's truck. He would come out and also give me a ride to class. Other nights I would crash at various friends' apartments.

One evening, I went to a party at the dorms with a guy I had met at the student union. That night was my first experience with drugs. I was naïve, and had no knowledge of drug use.

I had what he called a "sugar cube" and could not remember much after the drugs took effect. The guy who gave it to me said he could help me out with my homeless situation. All I had to do was trade sex acts in exchange for him finding me a comfy place. I never had intercourse; he was satisfied with oral sex. I am thankful I didn't have to continue these behaviors for too long.

Fortunately, I was given the opportunity to take over a lease from another friend of mine. I jumped at the chance. With only the clothes I packed, I moved right in. A couple weeks later, I found a classmate with a truck who helped me move the stuff from my parent's house to my new apartment.

My "drug connection" continued to provide me "happiness" for the same price as before, but now that I wasn't really in need, I made the decision to stop trading my body for drugs. Finally, my new life was starting. To celebrate my newfound home, my roommate and I had a party for the people in our apartment building. That's where I met the man of my dreams!

Chapter 7
THE ARMY WIFE

My new neighbor Michael came to our party, and he and I really seemed to hit it off. Everyone drank and had a great time, and after the party, I went to Michael's apartment. We talked straight through the night. Next thing I knew, it was time for my eight o'clock English class. Michael worked at the college and drove me to class.

A month went by and Michael asked me to be his girlfriend. I was nineteen and, at twenty-three, he was four years older than me. Many of his friends and especially his roommate were leery about our relationship and didn't trust me. I was still in the midst of starving myself and throwing up my meals. Michael's roommate noticed these behaviors and warned him that I was not a stable person. In his mind, I was somehow trying to use Michael for some unknown purpose.

At his friend's urging, Michael began to probe me about my past. Trying to explain all the things that got me to where I was at that moment can be too much for one person to take. I know he probably reconsidered his choice to date me, but he didn't stop. He stayed with me and, as a couple; we made plans for our future.

Michael was in serious training to join the Virginia State Police. He went for the physical and then was called back for the actual interview. Our plan was once he graduated from the police academy, we would get engaged and begin our new life wherever the police placed him.

The time came for Michael's interview. He asked me to accompany him on this trip, and I gladly went with him for support. I waited for several hours in his car for him to return. When I glimpsed Michael walking across the parking lot, I knew that his dreams of our life and the police academy were halted.

We went back to our hotel room and there, for the first time, we consummated our relationship. Michael made me a promise later that evening, he promised that we would spend the rest of our lives together, and I began to cry. I fell asleep next to the man I loved.

On our way home from Virginia, we stopped at a shopping mall to grab something to eat. We had decided the previous night that upon our return home, we would announce our engagement to our families. Now I just needed an engagement ring. We stopped at a few shops and then a decision had to be made. I looked at him and said, "I'll turn my back and you pick the one you think best represents your love for me."

Michael made the purchase, and we continued farther down the mall. When we came to a crowded food court, with a huge fountain right at the center, Michael picked me up and placed me on the fountain. All I was wearing was a sweatshirt and jeans. Completely taken off guard, I look down at Michael who had my ring. He shouted, "Faith, will you marry me?"

Totally blown away, I screamed, "yes," and jumped into

his arms. My fairy tale was finally coming true.

It didn't take long after our return for the word to get around about our engagement. Our families were surprised, but the response from Michael's friends came as no surprise. Several of them had private talks with me about the decision we were making. I did understand their concern. Michael and I had only known each other two months, and now we were engaged. Michael and I felt the same, but we knew we loved each other.

We still had some life decisions to make. I still had a long way to go before finishing school, and Michael needed to decide on a career. Working at the college and being a substitute teacher was fine, but he wanted more from life. Together we would figure this out. It felt great to be special to someone who wasn't trading my body to get something.

After much discussion, Michael and I came up with a wedding date: July 10, 1999. This was a mere eight months from when we were engaged. Since I was still in school full time, my mom and sister delegated themselves to work on the wedding details. When it came time for a decision, I made it, but their help was invaluable. It seemed our relationship was beginning to mend.

The day of the wedding was everything I'd dreamed it would be. My daddy walked me down the aisle and gave me away. My whole family was there to share in my happy day. Michael even had a surprise for me. He sang my favorite song "Wonder of Wonders" from "Fiddler on the Roof," and then at the reception he sang "How to Handle a Woman" from the musical "Camelot."

Our new life as husband and wife was beginning. As newlyweds, Michael and I made the decision that he would take steps to join the military. He underwent more training to prepare him for basic training, and just seven months after our wedding day, Michael left for basic training at Fort Benning, Georgia. As happy for him as I was, I felt so alone. My spiral was on its way down again.

Preparing for Michael's departure, I enlisted a roommate to help keep me company. Renae, who was also my carpool buddy at one time, agreed to move in with me. She had turned out to be a really close friend I could confide in.

After Michael left for basic training in February, my life turned upside down once again. His leaving threw me for a loop. I started drinking every night, and I even started my drug habit again. A friend I met in the theater department always had marijuana. Many nights she'd come over, and we would shut ourselves in my room and get drunk and high.

In one week my world really crashed. I was dealing with an increasingly strained relationship with Renae, because of my behavior, when, my best friend Tina's father died. Then an old friend that Renae and I both knew committed suicide, and my great aunt died from a rare form of cancer. All of my behaviors became increasingly worse, plus I started cutting again.

I controlled things the only way I knew how. I starved myself again. Now, right before Michael was due to graduate from basic training, I was a complete mess. I had to do something to keep from going crazy. Nothing seemed to be working; I needed my husband. He was the only person who could calm my fears.

Going to Michael's graduation was just what I needed. When I saw him dressed in his army uniform and glowing with pride, I knew that we'd be okay. I only had two semesters left of college, and then Michael and I would be off to Fort Knox. We would still be separated until I graduated college, but somehow everything would turn out so my life could continue to grow and flourish.

My college graduation could not come fast enough. Michael came up from Kentucky, and his parents also attended. Once again, no one from my family showed up for the commencement ceremony. However, there was a good reason for their absence. My brother's wife had just given birth to their son Zion, and he was not expected to live through his first week. My family was with my brother and his family to support them.

I packed up my car and headed south to Kentucky. I would finally be with my husband after what seemed like forever. Fort Knox brought its own stumbling blocks for Michael and me. Some, I thought for sure we would never get passed.

Once I got to Fort Knox, I was ready to be the doting army wife. I quickly became friends with other wives in the unit. We quickly settled into the post chapel, and not long after that, we found a nice home in a local community theater. I was so happy to be socializing with others. Being a wife was something I had always yearned for.

Chapter 8
THE RAPE VICTIM

In September 2002, just over a year after I moved to Kentucky, my world flipped upside down and inside out. There I was labeled with a new identity, "the rape victim."

I had wanted to get involved with the theater for so long, and I finally found a theater company near Fort Knox that I could take part in. I got the inclination to audition for a show "Crimes of the Heart." The director decided after the auditions that he didn't have everyone he needed to fill the roles, so he chose a different show, "The Women." For this show, he asked me to take one of the co-starring roles as a woman who was always pregnant. Ecstatic, I accepted the role and really began to feel at home.

"The Women" opened on Friday night, September 14, 2002. It was great! I loved it so very much. To celebrate our opening weekend, I decided to go to my favorite Karaoke spot and really live it up. What happened to me there forever changed the course of my marriage

To most people, fear, shame, guilt, anger, rage, and confusion are only emotions. For me, these are emotions I use to describe the way I felt after the night I was sexually assaulted, a night that would define my character.

September 14, 2002 was supposed to be a night to

celebrate. I never expected to have the memories I do about that night. I went out as I always did on a Saturday. I walked through the door at my favorite Karaoke spot and noticed everything was the same. I saw the DJ and the bartender and said, "Hello." I was comfortable. I was secure. I felt safe. This was a place where mostly everyone knew me. I couldn't have felt safer if I was in my own home with my husband. Feeling secure was the reason for my first mistake. I let my guard down. I felt invincible.

The friends I normally sang with didn't come out, so I decided to sit at the bar, something I had never done. I had always felt that sitting there was like broadcasting that you were there to pick up someone. The bar was so dead that night. I didn't think twice about sitting at the bar and talking to my friend who was bartending.

A man walked up beside me, put money on the bar, and began to charm me. This army reserve man never missed a beat. He started the conversation with showers of compliments. He told me I was beautiful, and that I had a singing voice like none he had ever heard. I was completely flattered. I was inexperienced when it came to men hitting on me, at least those without ulterior motives. I loved hearing these compliments. Sure, he said some things I didn't think were appropriate, but he was a man. When he asked me to go to a hotel, I informed him that I was married and I didn't want to do anything to damage the relationship I had with my husband. I also told him that just because I wouldn't go home with him, didn't mean we couldn't become friends and learn more about one another.

We started talking about his career in the army and the places we both had been. He showed me his nine tattoos, and I shared my personal information with him. He struck me as an average man who was trying to get some action. He compared what he could do to me to what my husband couldn't. He told me that after one night with him, I would never want to go back to my husband. I just reiterated how much I loved my husband and that we were happily married. That seemed to suffice for the time being.

He made other attempts to get with me. He tried a different approach each time. His last attempt was just before we left the bar when he said, "She is tempted, but still says no. Maybe I can convince her."

I looked him straight in his eyes and explained I was not in any way going to engage in that kind of activity while still married to my husband. He nodded in acknowledgement, and we continued our conversation.

The bar was soon closing, and his friends that had been sitting at a table behind us wanted to leave. They came over and asked if he was leaving with them, or if he could he get his own ride home. He looked at me. I figured that he needed a ride, so I offered to take him back to his barracks if he wanted to stay longer. He told his friends that I was driving him back and to go on ahead. This was my second mistake. How many people would give a ride to a person they had only known a few hours? Sadly, I am one of those people. I let our nice, easygoing conversation outweigh the inappropriate statements that had caused red flags to rise in my mind.

We stayed at the bar until the bartenders told us it was time leave the premises. I told this guy before we got into my car he had to tell me where he lived. I wasn't about to go wandering around the post with no idea of where I was going. He explained, in a way that I understood, where he lived, and I felt comfortable that I wasn't going to get lost or disoriented while trying to find his barracks.

At the barracks, I stopped to let him out of the car, politely told him good-bye, and wished him a safe trip back to Florida. He made one last effort to get me into bed, and I told him for the last time that I wasn't going to sleep with him and that it was better that we leave everything in a good way. He came over to my side of the car and proceeded to assault me. He inserted his hand inside of me and made me perform sexual acts on him.

What was I supposed to do now? Not only had this man violated me, he told me that I knew he had not done anything wrong. He kept telling me that what happened was a direct result of what he knew I wanted. I realized that I had a long road ahead of me if I decided to tell anyone.

When I got home, my husband was on the couch watching TV. I couldn't tell him what happened. I wasn't sure how he would react to me or to the situation. I tried to keep it to myself, but couldn't. Sunday night, less than twenty-four hours after I had initially been attacked, I told my husband. I couldn't live with this inside of me without breaking down. Mike was supportive and also firm about me reporting it.

On Monday afternoon, I went to the MP station and reported my rape. Agents from the Criminal Investigative Department (CID) took my statement. It was grueling. I was there for five and a half hours and incredibly scared. Many times, I had to stop while telling the story because I couldn't find the words to say what he did to me.

Soon after I gave my statement, they found the man and questioned him. The statement he gave almost matched mine perfectly. As part of the procedure, the accused is given the option of having a polygraph. He agreed to take one. He explained to the CID he wanted a polygraph to prove that even though I said, "No," he didn't really believe "No" is what I meant.

CID traveled to Florida to administer the test. As they were preparing to set up for the test, the accused gave a second statement. This statement was more detailed, and he actually stated that he knew I meant "No." He explained that I cried and was visibly shaking. I was under the impression that I was actually going to get what I wanted: justice. I didn't understand how far away justice really was.

The military justice system is different in many ways from the one that exists in the civilian world. When he was charged with my assault, he wasn't arrested. The military has strict guidelines about confining someone. He was allowed to continue with his life, even when he came to Fort Knox for a hearing. I was advised that if I saw him, I was supposed to leave wherever I was and find somewhere different to go. The irony was that I had to find somewhere else to go to avoid a confrontation when the man standing before me had been charged with forcible sodomy and indecent assault. It didn't seem fair. On the positive side, though, it doesn't take years to get situations like this resolved. From the time I was assaulted to the end of the trial was less than eight months. A civilian court would have probably taken years.

It was a hard road for me. I had to start going to counseling and taking medication to control the depression the situation caused. The trial was hard for me. I hated testifying about what happened. I knew that in order for me to get justice, I had to get up and tell my story. I had to be an example to those women who get attacked and never report it.

I made many mistakes during the attack, but the biggest ones were the things I didn't do when I was being attacked. I was always under the impression that simply telling a guy "No" and struggling was enough to show that I did not consent to what was happening to me. That is false. Unfortunately, for some in the military legal system, that isn't enough. During the trial, I wasn't able to prove force because I wasn't beaten and didn't leave any distinguishing scars on my attacker. The biggest decider for the judge was that I never honked the horn; I didn't bite him or scratch him. I made those decisions based solely on maintaining my own personal safety.

Although I couldn't prove force, we didn't come away empty handed. He was convicted of consensual sodomy and indecent acts. Those are the lesser-included charges of the original charges brought against him. It was hard for me to see this as a victory, but it was a victory nonetheless.

I can't say I have never regretted reporting the attack. There were many times when the prospect of not getting justice was too much for me to handle, but in the end, I know I did what I had to do for me. I couldn't stand by and let a man violate me and not have him punished. The thing that kept me moving forward was the support of my husband, and all of the people at the prosecutor's office who worked extremely hard on the case. They believed me, and they helped me see even with the mistakes that I made before and during the attack, I wouldn't be able to live with myself if I had made the biggest mistake of all: Not ever reporting the assault.

This assault did more to me after the fact than the horror of experiencing the trauma of the assault. I was plummeted into a manic stage like I've never known before.

So many men have preyed upon me in my life, and I had come to the end. I would no longer be anyone's prey. No, I would now prey upon them. I became a sexual predator.

I went back to the bars on post looking for men I could prey upon. I'd sit at the bar and survey the room. Each time I saw a lonely man, I'd make my way over and share drinks and small talk with him. Once I knew he was comfortable with me, I'd move in. I'd sweet-talk him and find out where he was staying. If he lived on post permanently, I couldn't use him; it would be too easy for us to run into one another somewhere else on post. If he was only there for training, a promotion, or school, I knew I was in the clear.

We'd go back to his place, and I would use him for sex. That's it. We'd have sex and while he went to clean up, I'd leave the room, without saying anything else to him. I repeated this act of "human hunting" nine separate times. Having sex with those men was an act of turning my guilt and shame outward. As vindicating as it felt at the time, I was being engulfed in rage and shame. This was, however, an apparent disregard for my marriage vows.

The last thing I wanted to do was disrespect my husband by putting him on the same predatory track I was on. To keep this from happening, I did not make love to Michael for months while this was going on. It was my way of protecting him. If I allowed myself to be intimate with him, it would forever cheapen our lovemaking. It couldn't have been easy for Michael to watch me spiral downward. Guilt engulfed me more and more as each day passed.

One night, as we were cuddling together on the couch, I finally broke. I began to sob. I saw the concern on my husband's face, and I couldn't keep my secret anymore. I reached over, grabbed the remote, and turned off the TV.

Tears were streaming down my face.

"I have something I have to tell you." I said.

"What happened?" he asked.

Through my tears I said, "I'm so ashamed. Please know how much I love you."

Looking a bit sterner he replied, "Did you sleep with someone else?"

"Yes, but it's not the way it seems." How many times have I heard that while watching movies on Lifetime? I was no better than an adulterer in one of those movies. Here I was groveling, hoping beyond hope that he would at least hear me out.

I recounted when all of these acts of unfaithfulness occurred and how many times. I was already prepared for the upcoming fallout. I went to my room and grabbed my suitcase. As I brought it out to the front door, Michael came to me, took my bag out of my hands, and gave me the longest heartfelt embrace that I have ever experienced. That single embrace made my tears flow even harder than before.

Once I calmed down enough, I asked him why he was so forgiving. Michael said, "Although I do not in any way condone the acts of unfaithfulness, I understand why it happened." He continued, "Faith, you went out looking for men that you could use like your rapist used you. This was your way of cutting yourself, but this time you used human beings to make the cuts for you and not a blade or knife."

This was a revelation I was not expecting to hear. It all made sense. This time instead of drowning in a depression, I was thrown into a whirlwind manic stage. I felt indestructible, and nothing in heaven or on Earth could bring me down.

I searched for a truth that couldn't be found in those

nine men I had vicarious sex with. My husband set me straight. I was still finding ways to self-destruct, but this time I was taking others down with me.

Michael and I, although still together, had a great deal of healing to do after this fiasco. I am still unsure if things will ever be the same for us again, because of the initial rape, and now because of the reality that I allowed myself to have unprotected sex with nine men that meant nothing to me. This would not be an easy row to hoe.

Chapter 9

THE BIPOLAR MOTHER

As much as Michael had forgiven me for what I had done to myself, to him, and to our marriage, he was having a difficult time now with the adjustment that had to be made. To our friends, and others in his unit, we put on a happy face, but underneath all those smiles and façades, there was a volcano brewing. Who knew when it would erupt?

July 2003, Michael and I went to Disney World to celebrate our fifth anniversary. It was just Michael and I, and we went to try and have fun. This was only a month or so after I had hunted for my last victim. Michael and I made love while we were in the "happiest place on Earth." It felt nice to know we could regain a modicum of normalcy with each other.

Two weeks after our return to Fort Knox, I was aware that my menstrual cycle was three days late. Just as I was getting ready to go out for a pregnancy test, my cycle began, but something was different this time. I could set my watch by my cycle, which was always on time. This time I was late, and once I started, the bleeding only lasted two days. I began to brood over this. The one thing I had been waiting for was a baby. Michael and I had been trying since May 2003. Every time I would get a bit excited at the prospect of being pregnant, reality would hit me. The last experience I had with a man I hunted and had sex with happened during the time Michael and I were trying. What if this wasn't our baby?

A few days later when I was certain my cycle was over, I took a pregnancy test. It read positive. I couldn't contain my excitement any longer. I called Michael at his unit to tell him the good news. When I told him and heard his response, my world came crashing down. "I can't be excited; it may not be mine."

I felt as if something had run me over. A cloud of mystery and secrets would surround my baby forever. I would always wonder about the father. I immediately started thinking of all those women on daytime talk shows who had four and five men lined up to take paternity tests. The worst part for me is that I never asked the names of my sex partners. I had no idea who any of my conquests were. A time that was supposed to be joyous and exciting was now my living nightmare.

I went to the hospital on post to have my blood tested to confirm my pregnancy and made my first appointment. At this appointment, I would find out how far along I was, which would be D-day for me.

The day of my appointment was filled with dread and the understanding that my marriage would probably be over if the timeline didn't fit when Michael and I had intercourse. I was shaking partly with anticipation and partly with excitement. Michael was pacing around the examination room, not unlike a new expectant father, but with a heavy heart as he waited to hear the news.

The nurse came into the room, and I felt as if I was

watching this happen from outside my body. Everyone and everything was moving in slow motion. I was sweating. My mind raced at the thought of having to eventually break the news to my family. This baby could be born under the darkness of what its mother had done. How could I raise a baby knowing that someone other than my husband had been responsible for the new life on Earth?

The moment of truth had finally arrived. The nurse pulled up my shirt and placed the gel on my stomach. As the probe traveled around the front of my abdomen, I wasn't breathing. I was holding my breath in hopes that somehow things would turn out all right.

It had been ten weeks since we returned from Disney World. The nurse diligently worked at taking pictures from all different angles to check the status of my precious cargo. At last, she spoke.

"You are ten weeks along." I breathed such a sigh of relief. I could see the worry wipe off Michael's face instantly. He came to my bedside and held my hand. We knew now that everything would be fine. Then the nurse spoke again. "This is only an approximate date. You could end up being as early as eight weeks and as far along as twelve. We just don't know a hundred percent."

As quickly as I had gone from worried to happy, my hopes were dashed. The knowledge that there wasn't a hundred-percent guarantee of my due date loomed over us. How could we be happy if we didn't know for sure? The only thing I could think to say to my husband, as the betrayal became evident on his face once again, was, "We'll take this one day at a time."

At my next appointment, I had to go over my genetic profiling. After all was said and done, I had to tell her about my unprotected sexual escapades, and that there was a question about paternity. She looked at me now with fire in her eyes. It was as if she heard the news from her own daughter. I was informed then that paternity could be determined after the baby was born, not news I wanted to hear. My husband and I would have to live with this uncertainty for nine very long months.

I made the decision that no matter the outcome, I would love this baby, and I was going to be happy. I prepared myself for the time when Michael would turn to me and say this was too much for him to handle. To be honest, I don't know a man alive who would forgive his wife after being told about nine separate acts of infidelity, let alone raise a child he knew might not be his. I was living life with Michael one day at time.

Other than Michael, the only person in my family who knew of my indiscretions was my baby sister, and she wasn't saying anything. Other than her, my family and friends were elated at the prospect of my becoming a new mother; I was not about to deflate their feelings by coming clean with them. To add to the joy, I found out my sister-in-law was also expecting, her third. Our kids would be just about two months apart.

I soon discovered I had another issue to add to my plate. Soon after moving to Kentucky, I touched base with my doctors. Since I had been diagnosed my senior year of high school with manic depression, the post physicians wanted to update my records to determine if I would be in need of behavioral health services.

In June 2001, I had gone to the clinic where the staff administered the psychiatric evaluation. My diagnosis was revised from manic depression, to bipolar and borderline personality disorder. I began a medication regime that consisted of Lithium. I knew the danger of this drug on my liver. At this point, Michael and I had not yet begun to try to get pregnant. In the two years prior to the pregnancy, the doctors had increased my dosage from 300 mg a day, to 1600 mg a day. They performed routine blood levels to make sure that the drug would not turn toxic in my system. It was working and my bipolar seemed to be under control.

When I discovered I was pregnant, I immediately stopped my medication and started my daily routine of prenatal vitamins. Nonetheless, my baby had been exposed to this drug for the first two months of my pregnancy. My doctor decided to keep an eye on my little one, and I was placed on the list of pregnant mothers whom they called "high risk."

I asked him what the risk factors would be if my unborn child had been exposed to this drug. He sat me down and said the most common side effect that they see in children who've been exposed is heart malformations. My heart dropped. On top of the knowledge that this child might not be my husband's, was the added anxiety that I had exposed my baby to this drug. Since I was deemed "high risk," my doctor performed many ultrasounds to check the formation of the heart. Unfortunately, there is only a small amount you can really see. Once again, to find out what damage was done, I would have to wait until my little one was born to know for sure.

My greatest fear, other than health issues, was that my child would turn out to be a boy. I knew that if I had a boy, it would be a slap in the face for my husband. To me, it would be clear as crystal the baby belonged to someone other than my husband. I prayed every night that my baby would be girl. I tried every superstition possible to ensure the gender of my little one. I just had to have a baby girl!

At seventeen weeks, my doctor did another ultrasound and informed us that our baby was undeniably a girl. Michael and I breathed a huge sigh of relief. We would name her Robin Elizabeth. As for her heart, the doctor could not see any major issues with it. A load was immediately lifted from our minds. In another twenty-two weeks, we would be the proud parents of a beautiful baby girl.

Those weeks went all too fast. Even without my medication, my pregnancy was relatively normal. My bipolar seemed to be held at bay, with all the other hormones my body was producing. I was enjoying the whole pregnancy. There were several times when I would stop and think about what having this baby would mean. I knew something that no one else knew about the last "hunt" I had been with: he was full-blooded Puerto Rican. I would know the moment this baby was born who the baby belonged to, even without a paternity test. If my darling baby came out with a different skin tone, my secret would be out.

Even up until the day of my delivery, no one other than me knew the ethnicity of the man I was with prior to our trip to Disney World. I really didn't see the point in telling anyone. It was just going to add to the burden Michael and I were carrying. I would know, and I was hoping my positive attitude would be enough to sway Michael from not having a paternity test.

I knew at my last appointment, that I was already 70 percent effaced. This baby was coming this weekend for sure. April 9, 2004 about 5:00 p.m., I began having pains in my stomach and thought my stomach was just upset.

They kept coming and became more and more severe. My dad finally made me realize that I was actually having contractions. My mom and dad got out pen and paper and were keeping track of their frequency.

At about 11:00 p.m., I couldn't stand it anymore. My contractions were getting stronger, but they weren't stopping. I wasn't getting a break from them. Michael packed me up and took me to the labor and delivery department at Ireland Army Community Hospital. I went into my room, and the doctor hooked me up to a fetal monitor and examined me. I was three centimeters dilated. The doctor told me I wasn't ready to give birth, gave me a Benadryl, and told me to go home and try to rest.

Like most first-time parents, we came home feeling a bit deflated at the "false alarm." After I came into the house and informed everyone that the baby wasn't coming yet, I took the other Benadryl, got into a very warm shower, and lay down to try and rest.

I could not get to sleep. My contractions were getting even sharper and harder to bear. I woke Michael up and said that I couldn't take this any longer. We got dressed and once again headed to the hospital.

When I showed up back on the ward, the doctor was not happy to see me. I explained how extreme the pains were and that even after a shower and two Benadryl, I still couldn't get enough relief to get any sleep. This time she admitted me. I got my IV in and was hooked up to the fetal monitor.

From the beginning of the pregnancy, I had told Michael that under no circumstances would I have an epidural. I wanted to have my first baby naturally. Well, once I started having these contractions, I knew I couldn't bear them for the 12–14 hours most first time mothers experience labor. I looked at Michael and told him that this wasn't the way it was supposed to be, and that I wanted an epidural. He asked me three times if I was sure. Emphatically, I made it known that I was going to get an epidural.

The anesthesiologist came by my room and set me up with an epidural. Once that was hooked up and flowing, I was comfortable enough to sleep. I was still only three centimeters dilated, and my water had not yet broken. I was left alone until the following morning.

At 8:00 a.m. on Saturday April 10, 2004, my doctor came in to examine me. He said he would let me go a while longer to see if my water would break on its own. "At 10:00 a.m. I will be back to see how you are doing, and if you haven't started hard labor, I will start it for you."

The time flew by. Before I knew it, 10:00 a.m. had arrived. My doctor came in and said I had progressed to five centimeters, but my water hadn't broken. He then got an instrument that can only be described as a very large crochet needle, and he broke my water.

Since I had the epidural, I couldn't feel anything. Michael, my mom, dad, and sister were all at the hospital and in my room with me up until this point. Once they broke my water, only my mom and husband remained. My nurses were constantly coming in and checking on my progress. Come 11:00 a.m., my nurse said, "Okay, we're going to do a practice push to see how far you will progress. You are probably going to be here a while, and we don't want you wasting all your energy."

Mom and Michael helped sit me upright, and I pushed for ten seconds. Once the push was over the nurse with a shocked voice said, "You can't push anymore or else the doctor will miss it. Don't push. The baby is crowning."

Shocked and excited I sat upright with my mom holding one leg and my husband holding the other, and I just wanted to push, but I couldn't. It seemed like it took forever for the doctor to return. Once he did, he grabbed the baby's head, I pushed two more times, and my precious baby girl was born. My beautiful Robin Elizabeth was born, and she had her mommy's skin, and Michael's nose. Any question I had about who the father of my baby was no longer mattered. I held her and loved her more deeply than I ever thought I was capable of loving anyone. I was a mother and a parent. I would be responsible for another human being, and she was perfect. She was my new beginning.

A few months after Robin's birth Michael hinted at wanting a paternity test. My heart dropped at the thought that he couldn't enjoy his daughter. However, he had every right to know the truth. If he really wanted it, I would agree to it, without question.

As Robin began to grow, she was no longer his little baby and had become his little girl. He could look at her and know in his heart that no matter what that test said, no matter what I said, that vibrant little girl was his daughter. No one could take that away. Michael's doubt washed away, and now we could really move on as a family.

In July 2005, Michael was honorably discharged from active duty in the reserves. We left Kentucky and made a new beginning in my hometown of Maidsville. My mom and dad had moved and started a new life in Ohio, and Kathy had gone with them to help out.

As life moved on, we changed with it. I was taking my medication; my daughter was thriving and was a blessing from God. Our lives dictated that we move back to Fairmont, so Michael and I found a house there that met the needs of our growing family. Joshua, my son, was already eight months old when we moved into our house. Things were going well, and we thought this would be it. We had put down roots and were comfortable in our new home. Robin was getting ready to start preschool, Josh was growing like a weed, I was doing well at my job at the local telecommunication outfit, and even Michael had a job at our college alma mater. Things couldn't have been any better.

Chapter 10
THE GRIEVING DAUGHTER

There are few times in our lives when we get a reality check. These checks of reality come in many forms. For my family and I, our reality check came on November 25, 2008, the day Michael lost his mom.

For the past nine years, Michael's mom had been such an inspiration not only to me, but to my kids as well. Given my history with my own grandparents, I was determined to change the pattern for my children. I made sure that both sets of grandparents got plenty of time to make memories with their grandchildren. Michael's parents came to visit us while we lived in Kentucky and during the summer brought the kids over to their house to have fun swimming and camping .

Robin and Patricia (Pat) were best buddies. Pat took Robin to day camp, on wagon rides around the neighborhood, and on walks by the river where Robin began her fascination with rocks. Joshua was just over a year old, but he had fun going trick-or-treating at the hospital where Pat was a diabetes educator. Pat loved her grandchildren. Her face lit up at the sound of their laughter and the pitter-patter of their feet running through her house.

For me, Pat was a second mother. My mother and I,

although not estranged, had a very strained relationship. I found much comfort in the idea of spending time with Pat. She and I had the relationship I always wanted with my own mom. I took every opportunity I could to be with Pat. She always treated me with respect and dignity. Just like in any relationship, we had our disagreements, mostly about child rearing, but she was always there to back up a decision I made concerning the kids. She was such an important part of mine and my children's lives and especially Michael's.

Although Michael favored his dad in looks, he had Pat's personality. He and his mom had the same kind of humor, and seeing their faces after they had made someone smile was priceless. I know he and his mom were close, although he'd never admit it.

On that horrible day in November, although I was working in a call center, I had made plans to go shopping on Black Friday with best friends Brandy and Pat. This would be the first time in several years that I didn't have to work on that day. I was putting in overtime during the week so I could afford to take off that day.

Tuesday, November 25, 2008, was a day just like any other. I got up early to start my overtime shift at work. Throughout the morning hours and into the afternoon, I wanted to talk to Pat to solidify our plans for Black Friday. I clocked out for my last break for the day at 2:15 p.m. I noticed I had several missed calls and voicemails from Pat's home number. Either she was calling or Dick, her husband, was trying to reach me. I listened to the voicemail. The voice on the recording was Dick's. "Faith, call me. Something's happened to Pat!" I immediately thought she had gotten ill with pneumonia or something and was probably in the hospital.

I finished getting my snack out of the vending machine

and dialed Dick's home number. Dick answered the phone, "Faith, Pat's dead she's been killed!" The last thing I remember was crying hysterically and members of my team lifting me up off the floor. This couldn't be true. Maybe I heard him wrong. How was I going to tell my daughter? How was I going to tell Michael? All these thoughts and many more were inundating my brain, and it hurt. How could this happen? I had many questions that needed answers, but first I had to tell Michael and the kids.

A close friend of mine from work drove me home. The kids came barreling down the steps wondering why I was home so soon. My friend took my kids back to her place for the afternoon so Michael and I could have some time to work things out. I had to tell Michael. How do you go about telling your husband his mother has been killed? There was no manual that could have prepared me for this kind of situation.

Like most men, Michael is not an emotional person. He is very centered and methodical. He adjusts quickly to changes, although he doesn't like change, and can often keep his cool when a situation turns chaotic. Needless to say, if I were ever in a natural disaster, Michael would be an indispensable member of my team. I knew that the strong façade that keeps him going on a daily basis was going to crumble.

I had to keep myself together to be strong for my husband in the wake of losing his mother. I knew that waiting wasn't the answer. I had to tell him now. "Michael, I need to talk to you. Something has happened."

In true Michael style he responded, "Just tell me. Don't sugarcoat it." I took a deep breath, exhaled, and said, "Your mom is dead. She's been killed in an auto accident." I went to his side, thinking he would need me to lean on, and then words came from his mouth I was not prepared to hear.

"Well, that stinks."

Michael was crushed. He just never allowed himself to show it. To this day, I've never seen him get emotional when talking about his mom, even though I know how close they were. I, on the other hand, was a wreck. I guess I was crying enough for the both of us. Michael and I now had to tell Robin.

Telling Robin was the hardest thing I have ever endured. I was not in charge of breaking the news to her. Michael volunteered and no one could have done it any better. It still breaks my heart into tiny shards to think of the look on my daughter's face when she realized her grandma, her best friend, was dead.

I was in no shape to comfort her. For a long while the three of us sat there. Robin sat between Michael and I and sobbed. Thankfully, my mom was there to help Robin. Robin talked to Nan Nan, and she seemed to do better.

The service was difficult. Robin cried and got her chance to say good-bye. My life was devastated. What was I going to do? I fell apart, but slowly pulled myself together and returned to work. This was the first time in quite awhile that my depression hadn't overwhelmed me. I was still on medications, and I'm so glad I was. Attempting to deal with this loss without them would have been tragic for me, because suicidal thoughts are present on a daily basis when you have bipolar and borderline personality disorder.

Even in the wake of the loss of my second mom, I was able to fight through the impulses to hurt myself. It's hard and it takes a great deal of will power, but I did it. I refused to allow myself to revert back to those behaviors.

Pat was well aware of my cutting issues. She never once condemned me for it. She was such an understanding soul. Knowing I had her approval meant everything to me. Each and every time I was about to harm myself, I thought of Pat. I looked at her face in a photo and knew exactly what she would say to me to ensure my safety. It would be years after her death before I would hurt myself again. However, once again, my life was changing. Only now, Pat wasn't with me to help me in person. I truly believe what happened in my life was a direct result of her helping me from heaven. I could only describe what happened as a result of the new changes as a miracle. Our family would now be given a new beginning in the aftermath of our family's loss.

PART 2

New Beginnings

Chapter 11
BEING SELF AWARE

After the death of my mother-in-law, my outlook on life changed. With her death, my family was given an opportunity to make a new beginning. Pat was with us for what seemed like a fleeting moment, but her outlook on life is what inspired me to start a new beginning.

Life is filled with beginnings. Birth, marriage, school, and even death are beginnings. Too often, we take for granted the opportunity that each beginning will provide for us. With each new beginning, there is something to learn that we can take with us for the duration of our lives. Seldom do we take a step back to discover the truths God is revealing.

God is very patient. He gently guides us to these lessons. If we don't get it the first time, well, that's okay. He is the omnipotent creator, and so he knows our human brain sometimes can miss opportunities to come. Since we didn't receive it the first time, he offers us yet another chance to take it all in. This cycle continues until what we need to learn is learned. Like I said, God is patient. He's much like a parent teaching their child to walk. At first, the child is wobbly and falls a good deal of the time. Eventually the child learns from his mistakes. As the parent, we hold our child's hand to help them up after a spill and get them started again. Each time, a lesson is learned, the child requires less and less from the parent. The same is true with our relationship with God. Each time we have to repeat a cycle, we take a little bit more from each lesson this cycle provides. Finally, we get all God wanted us to understand. As we go along, and learn these pearls of wisdom, others follow us in our lives. What we fail to understand is, maybe those that follow us are in need of a personal revelation. God places individuals in our lives so we can learn from their experiences. This also works the opposite way. We are placed in someone else's life so they too can have the opportunity to learn from our experiences.

Like many others, I've had to repeat cycles of lessons several times. Each time similar circumstances arose, I found myself laughing. Sometimes I will look up into the sky and say, "Really God?" However, I never learned what I was supposed to. I was determined to think that this repeated lesson was a punishment.

Learning lessons is never an easy thing. Never. Life is full of opportunities for learning. We just have to open our eyes and hearts to the teachings God has for us. It's not just listening. We must be willing to put all we've learned into action and let it have the impact God intended.

I am a mother and a wife with bipolar and borderline personality disorders. Relationships are difficult on their own without the added distraction of mental illness. After what I have persevered through, I promised God and myself I was going to be the mother I always wanted my mom to be. My children would never have bad or hurtful memories of their grandparents. That not only became my ultimate goal, but my ultimate obsession as well. Protecting my little ones from having a life like mine was the prize at the end of the long race. I wasn't doing a very good job.

I still didn't have a decent relationship with my own mother, so how was I supposed to ensure a different outcome for my children, one that guaranteed that my kids had a loving and growing support system.

My plan became my obsession and was consuming me. I had forgotten a very important part of the plan to make it a reality: taking care of me. I was not a mentally healthy person. In the same fashion as most bipolar sufferers, my medication regime was pretty much non-existent. Not long after Pat passed away, I quit taking my medication. The largest problem for me when I'm without my medication is that my ability to control my impulses is terribly diminished.

I'm most fearful of my rage. My greatest fear is that in a fit of frustration or anger, I will end up hurting one or both of my children. The day that I would have to come face-to-face with that reality came all too quickly. After my daughter was born, I wrestled with the question, Should I tell her about my condition? I was avoiding the day as long as I possibly could. I never wanted to have to explain why mommy had to take medicine everyday.

From a very young age, Robin had a level of understanding far beyond her years. I knew this for sure when Pat died. Most children of four don't fully comprehend death the way adults do. Robin understood it. I saw her go through the grieving process, one step at a time. When it came time to sit down and have the conversation about mommy's illness, I knew if I tried to sugarcoat anything, she would pick up on it.

Robin was only six years old when I was forced to have

the Mommy's-brain-is-sick talk. It came about because she began to notice my behaviors changing. One day I'd be happy and smiling and the next, who knows? This upset and confused her. She came to me with tear-filled eyes and said, "Mommy, what did I do to make you so unhappy?" As my own eyes let go of tears, I explained that Mommy's brain doesn't allow her to deal with things the right way. She and I sat on the couch for a long while and had a very productive conversation. I made a decision. I knew just how to help us both get through this with as little damage as possible.

My cycles happen on a fairly regular schedule. I will deal with one cycle between 4–6 weeks. Since I am aware of my transitions, I can fully make her aware of these changes. If I am in a manic stage, where many things easily frustrate me, I can use a "special phrase" to let Robin know that Mommy's brain is working a bit differently. "I need some space," are the four words I decided to use as Robin's cue to keep her distance. This lets her know that she and Joshua are not at fault, and that Mommy needs some alone time. It gives me a safe way to escape from where my mind takes me.

For so long, I wanted to hide my disorder. I was fearful that it would do more damage. From this new beginning, I learned I didn't give my daughter or my God enough credit. I also came out with the knowledge that I didn't have to suffer in silence anymore.

Chapter 12
THE RESPONSIBLE DECISIONS

Once you become self-aware, making difficult decisions seems to be easier. Being responsible is sometimes the hardest part. Not everything is going to be clear-cut. The responsible decisions are the most difficult to make because they seldom have easy answers.

To admit you cannot fulfill a commitment because you know that not fulfilling it is the best decision for all those involved is the worst. Living with the knowledge that you are not emotionally equipped to handle things is difficult. Having it become public knowledge, and possibly a public embarrassment is even more so. However, it is much more responsible to concede before the commitment, than to try and take on a responsibility you aren't ready for.

When my children were seven and four, I had a decision to make. I could either ignore the fact that being off my medicines would cause me to act erratically and perhaps effect my ability to care for my children, and potentially lead to harming them; or I could accept I wasn't in a place where I could keep them safe and allow a trusted family member to care for them.

To many, this was a clear-cut decision. For me it was gut wrenching. I really wanted to be the mother they needed me to be. I could suppress my emotions and do my motherly duty, but at what cost? If I ignored the signs of my impending breakdown and the risk of my unintentionally hurting them, I would be in for a host of consequences. On the other hand, what kind of parent allows a child to be cared for by someone else? As their mother, it would be selfish to pawn my kids off on someone else just so I could have some "Me" time.

It didn't matter. I still had a choice to make. I made the choice to allow Dick, my father-in-law, to watch my kids for three weeks. I made plans to go to Washington and visit a really close friend of mine. I came to the conclusion that in order for me to truly be the mother my kids needed, I had to first allow myself some healing. If I could not be responsible enough to properly care for myself, there would be no way I could be responsible for affectively caring and nurturing my two children.

Many saw my decision as one made from pure selfishness. They truly felt it was the wrong decision; one they would have made differently. At another time in my life, knowing the decision these others would have made in the same situation would have devastated me. Not now. My personal revelation was that I couldn't allow others to dictate what was best for my family and for me. I know I made the right choice at the right time. Although it was hard, I did what was best and necessary. Now that I have the ability to make the responsible decisions, I can also admit when I am over my head, and with this, comes the knowledge that I prevented a tragedy.

Chapter 13
THE JOURNEY IS
SOMETIMES LONELY

You may be starting your new beginning, but that doesn't' mean that those in your life will be taking the trip with you. The start of your new journey may feel like going on a first date, new and refreshing. However, as time goes on, the newness will wear off, especially in the face of old habits.

For me, my journey started to lose its newness as I dealt with my younger sister. Our relationship was tedious at best. I saw in her something that I always wanted, a loving relationship with our grandmother. To help this all fit together, I will tell you a little story.

When I was young, maybe around six or seven, my grandmother uttered words that totally devastated me to my core. "I don't love you! I don't want you!" She never changed her feelings about me, even when she was battling cancer, and my family and I never understood why. Even after that, I was bound and determined to change her mind but couldn't. On the contrary, the more I did to prove my love and worth, the more hate spewed from her, as she beat and starved me.

My sister has never uttered these awful words to me or

beaten me the way my grandmother did, but my sister did have the undying love and devotion. Given the opposite sides my sister and I lived on, growing up together was filled with rejection and non-reciprocating love from her.

Approaching adulthood, I continued my quest to prove my love and devotion to my sister. I drove eight hours to get her after she left our parent's house; I helped her find a job and an apartment. I also loaned her my cell phone, so she could have a point of contact for her job. All of this was met with greed and disdain, if I was unable to help her later.

How could all of this love and care go virtually unnoticed and unappreciated? I still have no answer. I have accepted that I will never see any of the money she owes me, and I don't expect her habits to change. My baby sister is the closest link I have to my grandmother. Somewhere in my heart, I truly believe that if I can find acceptance in my sister's eyes, then maybe I can achieve a belated sense of love and approval from my grandmother.

Somehow, I lost my focus on why I was doing things for my sister. Now I realize that I was doing it more to get approval from her rather than to help her because I wanted to. The truth is, it was a little bit of both. I wanted to help in any way I could, but in the back of my mind, I was secretly hoping to magically receive that love and approval I'd been craving for so long. This is when I realized that the journey to my new beginning was one I would have to take alone.

Chapter 14
CHANGING MY PATTERNS

The journey of my new beginning is first learning that I cannot change others. I can only change myself. I am taking the steps to learn how not to engage in those fruitless habits. I am starting by changing my communication patterns. If someone I have an unhealthy relationship with begins to draw me into patterns that I have been comfortable in before, I will be able to take control of the conversation. Sooner or later, the change I've made in myself will inevitably change the relationship I have with everyone. The ball is now in my sister's court. She can accept the changes or not, either way I am moving forward.

As you begin your new journey, or continue on it if it's already started, the most important thing to remember is to not let others in your life keep you from your new beginning. Those around you will eventually come to a crossroads. They have a choice; they could either go with you on this journey, or choose another road where you will both part company.

Don't be too discouraged if others aren't ready to join you. Seeing a positive change in you may spark in them a journey to their new beginnings. When they start their journey, at some point, your paths may cross again, but this time with new authority and power, and better yet, a regaining of God's identity, the one you were always meant to have.

Chapter 15
MY GOD-GIVEN IDENTITY

I do not have a specific name for the identity that God has given me. I know he knows what it is. I really believe that I may never figure out that identity. I do, however, know what I'm not.

I learned from a friend of mine that much like anyone with an illness, I began to identify myself as that disease. I would often introduce myself as, "Faith, I am bipolar." Although I never said it like that, it is still how I identified myself. Bipolar and borderline personality disorders ruled my life. Those two disorders were what dictated what I did and how I did them. Many times, I turned down opportunities because I believed having bipolar and borderline were somehow a roadblock that kept me from participating in certain activities.

There was still a stigma on people like me that suffer from bipolar and borderline disorder. I worked very hard to make sure that the people I worked with had no idea about my conditions. If they knew that I was suffering from a mental illness, it would change the way they interacted with me, and I couldn't bear that.

Prior to the birth and pregnancy of my son, Joshua, I worked as the assistant manager for a women's retail store.

I worked very hard to learn everything I could about the store. I had a wonderful rapport with my co-workers and district manager. I knew there was a great deal of detail that had to be executed in various areas throughout the store, and my goal was to gain proficiency in each area.

I have always given 110 percent on the job. Inevitably, I started to cycle through to a manic stage. I still was not taking my medications, so that just made everything worse. I still gave all I had, but I was becoming impulsive. I was buying things from the store on a daily basis. I was using the store credit card to make my purchases so Michael wouldn't know. On top of that, I began to cut again.

Every Tuesday, our store would get its shipment for the week. As we opened the boxes, I was thinking about cutting. I took one of the box cutters from the shipment, placed it in my purse, and used it to cut myself. My injuries started to show. I used a story to cover it up, but one of my co-workers recognized the behaviors. In an attempt to help me, she reported me to my store manager, and I was no longer permitted to help with shipments. The district manager was made aware. I did not know she knew and had ordered the store manager to keep all of those things locked up in a safe place where I did not have access.

A few weeks later, my store manager announced she was leaving the company for a job closer to her home. I was excited because that meant I would be able to move up into a salaried position. To run my own store would be so wonderful. The district manager came by to interview me along with several others for the position. I was told that the company preferred to hire inside the company, so my wish to move up was almost inevitable.

I never received my promotion. My district manager

pulled me into the back office and said that upper management didn't believe that I was mentally ready to handle such a job. I knew right then that my cutting was made public, and there would be no way around it. I decided to take my fate in my own hands and found myself a new job. I would be assistant manager in another women's clothing retail chain. This job did not end happily either.

Two weeks after I left one job to enter another, I discovered I was pregnant with Joshua. I worked hard and even volunteered to work weekends and holidays. At that time, Robin was so young that it wouldn't matter to her one way or another. As usual, I gave all I had and more to make myself a success in the eyes of my manager. One day, my being bipolar came out in a conversation. After that, my store manager wasn't quite sure how to handle me. I could tell she was mulling over the things she'd heard about people who suffer from my condition.

When it came time to leave to have Joshua, the girls I worked with gave me a huge basket of baby items and sent me on my way. Everyday they asked when the baby was coming and if I had gone into labor. For this pregnancy, I had to request a leave of absence since I had not been with the company for a full year. This meant I could later return in my current capacity.

Exactly eight weeks after Joshua was born, I called my manager, and she had informed me she had just hired some new people and didn't have room to keep me. I knew then it had nothing to do with them being full, and more to do with her not wanting to work with someone like me.

Believe it or not, it was the best thing. I didn't see it then, but her ignorance gave me an opportunity that I never had with Robin; I could stay at home and take care of my kids while Michael worked. That was the one thing I wish I could have done with Robin, but it hadn't worked out that way.

One thing to remember on your journey to a new beginning is that there are opportunities everywhere to learn and gather valuable information. Take each and every one of those opportunities and bask in them; you never know what will come of them. I took advantage of such an opportunity.

Michael's sister was talking to one of her friends and mentioned that I was an interpreter for the deaf. Her friend told her to tell me to get an application in right away. I did; In June 2009, I interviewed with a regional agency that supplies school systems with interpreters and other services. After my interview, I was told I got the job. My family was moving from Fairmont to Weirton, West Virginia, and I would be interpreting for a student in one of the schools.

In less than a month, we had found and closed on a house. We didn't have a mortgage and owned our house free and clear. Robin and I started in our respective schools, and this is where my life has brought me today.

Weirton, West Virginia is a very small town, but it was once huge, when the steel mill was still open. I am amazed at the quality of people who live here. We found Cove; a church attended by so many amazing people. It didn't take us long to transfer our membership to this church, a place where I truly made my new beginning.

My pastor was with me for the miscarriage of my baby and the chaos that ensued after. I wanted to die. I was ready to kill myself. I told my minister this and he said, "You are too important for God or I to let go. I'm not letting go."

Those words still cause shivers down my spine. To know I'm not alone. Wow!

I once started this journey alone and in solitude. My new beginning now starts with a circle of friends that I could never replace. Most importantly, I have a new understanding of God's grace and mercy. His mercies are renewed every morning. As much as I change, he never does. He remains the same today, yesterday, and forever. My new beginning truly started with my new relationship with Christ.

Chapter 16
A Relationship with Christ

For centuries, Christianity and other religions in the world had many denominations. This can make it very confusing for someone who is searching for the truth. All of these denominations do hold truth, but whether it's the truth is up for debate. For this reason, it is best not to search for the truth inside churches but to look in your heart. If you are unsure about what you believe, talk to someone close to you that you admire.

I am a Christian, and there are many times I find myself questioning my beliefs. That is a good thing. If you are asking questions, it means you are coming closer and closer to your own personal revelation of God. What follows is a personal relationship with God. A personal relationship with God is the only thing that God asks of us to get to heaven. If you don't know him personally, you can't be close to him. The good news, my friends, is that God is always there. He has always been there. He has never left us, even though we didn't realize he was there.

You may be asking yourself, "How do I get this personal relationship with God?" Well, you need to pray to God and simply tell him you're lost and you don't know what else to do. Tell him you want him to be in your life guiding you.

God will never turn down an honest plea for mercy.

God is merciful and showers us with grace everyday. Any time you have a question, he's listening to your heart. Even if you don't know the words to say, just pray in silence. God will hear you and the desires of your heart. I'm not saying it is going to be easy. Change is never easy, especially when you are trying to change old habits. I promise you, though, if you can continue to allow God to shape you, you will become the best "you" he created you to be. You will have trials. You will doubt your faith. You will doubt that God is there.

Hebrews 11:1 Faith is the substance of things hoped for and the evidence of things not seen.

Faith isn't easy. It requires you to really trust that God knows what he's doing. The amazing thing is that God is always in control. If we simply give him control of our lives, we will be filled with satisfaction and joy like we've never known.

An important thing to remember is that although we will experience bad days, days where we feel we just can't go on, we just need to remember that God is never going to let us go. We are his children, and we are all important to Him. Even if you have to say it to yourself over and over, he will grant you peace, and he will finish the work he started in you.

I said before that I didn't have a specific name for the identity that God has for me. I'd like to take that back. My new identity is "child of God." If I can identify myself as a child of God, then everything else will follow.

As you finish reading this, I pray that God moves through you to get you started on your own journey to your new beginning Then you'll be able to find your God-given identity.